D0990786

New Jersey

BY M. J. YORK

The Child's World

Published by The Child's World®
1980 Lookout Drive • Mankato, MN 56003-1705
800-599-READ • www.childsworld.com

ACKNOWLEDGMENTS
The Child's World®: Mary Berendes, Publishing Director
The Design Lab: Design and production
Red Line Editorial: Editorial direction

PHOTO CREDITS: Shutterstock Images, cover, 1, 3; Matt Kania/Map Hero,
Inc., 4, 5; George Olsson/iStockphoto, 7; Aimin Tang/iStockphoto, 9; 123RF,
10; Michael Hare/Shutterstock Images, 11; Robert Essel NYC/Photolibrary,
13; North Wind Picture Archives/Photolibrary, 15; judywhite/Photolibrary, 17;
Scott Heppell/AP Images, 19; Kordcom/Photolibrary, 21; One Mile Up, 22;
Quarter-dollar coin image from the United States Mint, 22

Copyright © 2011 by The Child's World®
All rights reserved. No part of this book may be
reproduced or utilized in any form or by any means
without written permission from the publisher.

LIBRARY OF CONGRESS CATALOGING-IN-PUBLICATION DATA
York, M. J., 1983–
    New Jersey / by M.J. York.
        p. cm.
    Includes index.
    ISBN 978-1-60253-474-2 (library bound : alk. paper)
    1. New Jersey—Juvenile literature. I. Title.

F134.3.Y67 2010
974.9—dc22

                                    2010018654

Printed in the United States of America in Mankato, Minnesota.
July 2010
F11538

On the cover:
Steel Pier is
an amusement
park in Atlantic
City, New
Jersey.

LeRoy Collins Leon Co.
Public Library System
200 West Park Avenue
Tallahassee, FL 32301

CONTENTS

974.9 YOR
1665-7416 9/17/2012 LCL
York, M. J., 1983-

New Jersey.

Geography

Let's explore New Jersey! New Jersey is in the eastern United States. It is next to the Atlantic Ocean.

CONNECTICUT

NEW YORK

PENNSYLVANIA

Ridgewood

West Orange

Newark

Jersey City

NEW YORK

New Brunswick

Trenton ★

Delaware River

Camden

Browns Mills

Atlantic Ocean

NEW JERSEY

MARYLAND

Bridgeton

Millville

Newport

DELAWARE

Atlantic City

Ocean City

NORTH
WEST · EAST
SOUTH

Delaware Bay

Cape May

Cities

Trenton is the capital of New Jersey. An important battle was fought here during the **American Revolution**. Newark is the state's largest city. Camden and Jersey City are other well-known cities.

Newark is home to more than 280,000 people. ▶

Land

Beaches and **marshes** are along New Jersey's long coast. The state has many rolling hills. It also has mountains in the northwest. New Jersey's western border is the Delaware River.

A bridge over the Delaware River connects New Jersey to Pennsylvania. ▶

Plants and Animals

New Jersey's state animal is the horse. The state flower is the violet. The state bird is the eastern goldfinch. New Jersey also has a state dinosaur: the *Hadrosaurus*. It was the first dinosaur **fossil** found in the United States.

Violets are often purple. ▶

New Jersey's state shell is the knobbed whelk. This type of shellfish can be found on every beach in the state.

People and Work

New Jersey is home to nearly 8.7 million people. Most people live in cities. Some work in jobs that serve the people who visit the state's beaches and **boardwalks**. Some people in New Jersey make medicine or **chemicals**. Farmers in New Jersey grow berries, peaches, apples, and lettuce.

New Jersey is home to companies that produce drugs for medical use. ▶

History

Native Americans have lived in the New Jersey area for thousands of years. Then, settlers came from Europe. The **Dutch** first claimed New Jersey in the 1600s. Then, the land was ruled by England. New Jersey was one of the 13 original **colonies**. On December 18, 1787, New Jersey became the third U.S. state.

During the American Revolution, more battles took place in New Jersey than in any other colony.

American troops fought against the British during the American Revolution. ▶

Ways of Life

Many people visit New Jersey's beaches. They walk on the boardwalks. They eat ice cream, saltwater **taffy**, and pizza. They go shopping. They play games and ride roller coasters.

New Jersey boardwalks have games, rides, and food. ▶

ANIMAL
HOUSE

17

Famous People

U.S. President Grover Cleveland was born in New Jersey. Woodrow Wilson was governor of New Jersey before he became president of the United States. Musicians Bruce Springsteen and Frank Sinatra were born in New Jersey, and the Jonas Brothers were raised in the state.

Inventor Thomas Edison did a lot of his work in New Jersey.

The Jonas Brothers are a **popular** music group from Wyckoff, New Jersey. ▶

Famous Places

For more than one hundred years, people have visited Atlantic City in New Jersey. The first boardwalk in the country was built there in 1870. It is one of the most popular places for **tourists** in the United States.

In Atlantic City, visitors can fish, shop, play golf, and visit the beach. ▶

State Symbols

Seal

The New Jersey state seal has a horse and a helmet. These stand for New Jersey's **independence**. Go to childsworld.com/links for a link to New Jersey's state Web site, where you can get a firsthand look at the state seal.

Flag

The seal is on the state flag. The flag shows two women. One woman stands for liberty. The other woman stands for farming.

Quarter

New Jersey's state quarter shows George Washington crossing the Delaware River. The quarter came out in 1999.

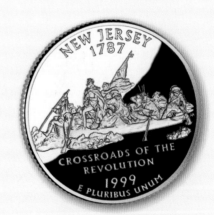

Glossary

American Revolution (uh-MER-ih-kin rev-uh-LOO-shun): During the American Revolution, from 1775 to 1783, the 13 American colonies fought against Britain for their independence. Many battles of the American Revolution were fought in New Jersey.

boardwalks (BORD-woks): Boardwalks are wooden sidewalks built along a shore. Many people visit New Jersey's boardwalks.

chemicals (KEM-uh-kulz): Chemicals are substances used in chemistry. Some people in New Jersey work to make chemicals.

colonies (KOL-uh-neez): Colonies are areas of land that are newly settled and controlled by a government of another land. There were 13 original British colonies in America.

Dutch (DUCH): Dutch means from the Netherlands, a country in Europe. The Dutch first claimed New Jersey.

fossil (FOSS-ul): A fossil is the remains of an animal or plant that lived millions of years ago. The first dinosaur fossil found in the United States was found in New Jersey.

independence (in-deh-PEN-denss): Independence is freedom. The American colonies fought for independence from Britain during the American Revolution.

marshes (MARSH-ez): Marshes are wet, low lands. There are marshes in New Jersey.

popular (POP-yuh-lur): To be popular is to be enjoyed by many people. New Jersey boardwalks are popular places to visit.

seal (SEEL): A seal is a symbol a state uses for government business. New Jersey's seal has items that stand for independence.

symbols (SIM-bulz): Symbols are pictures or things that stand for something else. Symbols for the state are on New Jersey's seal and flag.

taffy (TAF-ee): Taffy is a sweet, chewy candy that is boiled and stretched. New Jersey is known for its saltwater taffy.

tourists (TOOR-ists): Tourists are people who visit a place (such as a state or country) for fun. Tourists visit New Jersey to see the beaches and boardwalks.

Further Information

Books

Cameron, Eileen. *G is for Garden State: A New Jersey Alphabet*. Chelsea, MI: Sleeping Bear Press, 2004.

Evento, Susan. *New Jersey*. New York: Children's Press, 2004.

Keller, Laurie. *The Scrambled States of America*. New York: Henry Holt, 2002.

Web Sites

Visit our Web site for links about New Jersey: *childsworld.com/links*

Note to Parents, Teachers, and Librarians: We routinely verify our Web links to make sure they are safe and active sites. So encourage your readers to check them out!

Index